A MESSAGE FROM JACQUELINE

Tracy's thrilled to bits to have her very own quiz book! I do hope you enjoy reading all about her. I've had a go at answering all the questions myself and I'll tell you something funny. I've often got the answers wrong — even though I invented Tracy! Still, she does seem to have taken on a life of her own. She's a terrible show-off at times and can frequently behave atrociously — but I do love her, and I hope you do too.

Jacqueline Wilson

www.jacquelinewilson.co.uk

Jacqueline Wilson

THE TRACY BEAKER QUIZ BOOK

Illustrated by Nick Sharratt

CORGI YEARLING

THE TRACY BEAKER QUIZ BOOK
A CORGI YEARLING BOOK 978 0 440 86891 0

Published in Great Britain by Corgi Yearling,
an imprint of Random House Children's Books
A Random House Group Company

This edition published 2009

1 3 5 7 9 10 8 6 4 2

Illustrations copyright © Nick Sharratt, 1991, 1992, 1993, 1994,
1995, 1996, 1997, 1998, 1999, 2000, 2001, 2002, 2003,
2004, 2005, 2006, 2007, 2008, 2009

The right of Jacqueline Wilson to be identified as the author
of this work has been asserted in accordance with the
Copyright, Designs and Patents Act 1988.

Text written by Alexandra Antscherl
Designed by Becky Chilcott

Set in Blueprint

Corgi Yearling Books are published by Random House Children's Books,
61–63 Uxbridge Road, London W5 5SA

www.kidsatrandomhouse.co.uk

Addresses for companies within The Random House Group Limited
can be found at: www.randomhouse.co.uk/offices.htm

THE RANDOM HOUSE GROUP Limited Reg. No. 954009

A CIP catalogue record for this book is available
from the British Library.

Printed and bound in Great Britain
by CPI Bookmarque, Croydon, CRO 4TD

CONTENTS

A MESSAGE FROM TRACY BEAKER

Hi! Welcome to this ultra-cool Tracy Beaker Quiz Book. You are in for the treat of your life. How much do you know about me? If you can answer all the fun questions in this book then you can consider yourself my Number One Fan!

Don't fuss if you get stuck once or twice. I'm an exceedingly complex character and I've led an action-packed life. Even Elaine the Pain doesn't know every single Tracy Beaker statistic and she's got a file about me that's THIS thick. Take that as a challenge if you like. In fact, I *dare* you to see how many questions you can answer. Enjoy learning all about the truly terrific, talented Tracy Beaker. Go on — give yourselves a treat!

Tracy xxxxxxxx

HOW TO HOST YOUR OWN TRACY BEAKER QUIZ PARTY

You can dip in and out of this book, on your own or with your mates, whenever you like, but why not invite a few friends round for a special Tracy Beaker Quiz Party? Here's some suggestions to make a special occasion out of it.

☆ VENUE ☆

Get a room to yourselves – This might have to involve bribing your brother or sister to go elsewhere if you share a bedroom. See notes about snacks below for handy bribe ideas!

Get comfy – Cushions, beanbags or sleeping bags on the floor will help. Cardboard furniture as made by Alexander in *The Dare Game* probably will not!

Decorate – Make it party time with streamers and balloons. A tablecloth on the floor adds to the festive feel – and makes it much easier to clear up the crumbs afterwards! You could draw your favourite Jacqueline Wilson characters and hang the pictures round the room. Or pick a room to copy such as Tracy Beaker's bat-cave bedroom – but don't paint your room black without asking first!

☆ FOOD ☆

Snacks — Lay in serious supplies of your best snacks. Tracy Beaker's favourites are Smarties and cake, but you might have other ideas. Crunchy carrot and cucumber sticks feed the brain better — and balance out the snacks a bit! You could have a go at making the fairy cakes with the recipe on page 102. A good mixture of sweet and savoury, healthy and treats will mean there's something to tempt everyone.

Drinks — Keep the brain well watered to help you with the quiz. Tracy Beaker prefers strawberry milkshake. What do you like best? Don't forget plenty of cups and straws for your friends.

☆ EQUIPMENT ☆

Appoint a quiz master, maybe the host of the party, to read out the questions and write down the scores for each round on the special score sheets on pages 123–7. Everyone will need a pen and notepad each for writing down the answers.

Remember, there's no need to do all 16 quizzes in one session, and you don't have to do them in the order they appear in the book.

☆ DRESS UP ☆

You could invite your friends to come in costume, as their favourite characters from the Tracy Beaker stories. Will you get five different Tracys? Or will some people be more original? After the quizzes, why not act out the fabulous play script on page 84?

☆ PRIZES ☆

Your friends will be thrilled if you give out little prizes at the end. Don't limit it just to the person with the highest score though. Why not also award a prize for most original answer in quiz 16, or one for best costume, quickest person to complete a round, or fastest fairy-cake muncher?

☆ SLEEPOVER ☆

If you're seriously lucky, you might be able to turn the whole event into a sleepover. You'll probably have time to cook the recipe on page 94 for your dinner and do the puzzles and some pen and paper games, as well as the quizzes. Just add sleeping bags, pyjamas and lots of late-night, lights-out giggling!

☆ ☆ ☆ Quiz 1 ☆ ☆ ☆

THE STORY OF TRACY BEAKER

Test your knowledge of the first book about Tracy

1. What is Tracy writing in this book?

. . . .

. . . .

2. What was the name of the doll that Tracy's mum gave her when she was little?

. . . .

. . . .

3. Which cartoon character is on Justine's special clock?

. . . .

4. What is Peter doing when Tracy sees him on the landing in the middle of the night?

. . . .

. . . .

5. What does Tracy do before Cam's first visit to the children's home?

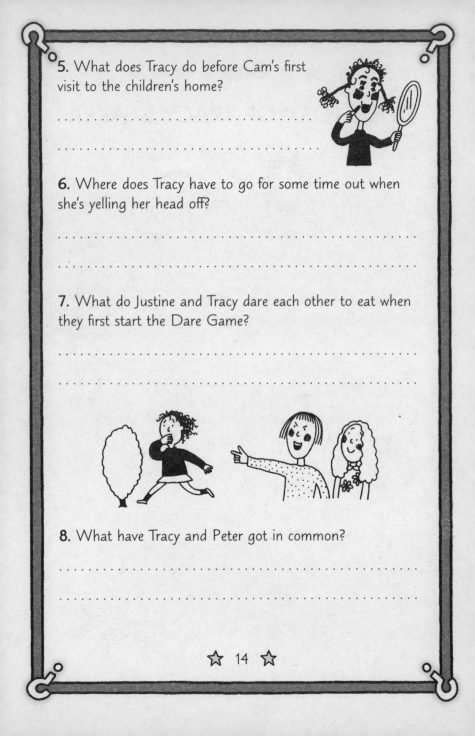

....

....

6. Where does Tracy have to go for some time out when she's yelling her head off?

....

....

7. What do Justine and Tracy dare each other to eat when they first start the Dare Game?

....

....

8. What have Tracy and Peter got in common?

....

....

9. What sort of games does Peter like to play with Tracy?

....

....

10. Which two girls sneak a look at Tracy's life story book when Tracy goes to help in the kitchen?

....

....

11. Who gave Justine her alarm clock?

....

....

12. Is there a pet at the Children's Home?

....

....

13. What form of transport does the Home have?

. . . .

. . . .

14. What sort of car does Tracy imagine
her mum has?

. . . .

. . . .

15. When Tracy wants to 'phone home' it reminds her of a
character from a film. Which one?

. . . .

. . . .

16. What does Tracy give to Justine at the
end of the book?

. . . .

. . . .

STARRING TRACY BEAKER

*Do you know what happens when Tracy
has a chance to shine as an actress?*

1. Which play is Tracy's school putting on?

. . . .

. . . .

2. Which part is Tracy given?

. . . .

. . . .

3. Why does Tracy want to make a special Christmas
punch drink?

. . . .

. . . .

4. Can you name the four presents Tracy sends her mum
for Christmas?

. . . .

. . . .

5. What does Tracy do to Justine when she's winding Tracy up about her mum not coming to the play?

....

....

6. What does the headmistress then ban Tracy from doing?

....

....

7. What do the social workers at the Dumping Ground get Tracy to do 'to channel her aggression'?

....

....

8. Who organizes the other kids into helping Tracy with her new job?

....

....

....

....

....

9. What does Peter do to try to get Tracy back in the play?

. . . .

. . . .

10. What two costumes does Tracy have for her part as Scrooge?

. . . .

. . . .

11. Which part does Peter play?

. . . .

. . . .

12. What does Tracy's mum send her after the play?

. . . .

. . . .

Congratulations, my little star.
Wish I could have seen you.
Lots of love, Mum xxx

13. What sporting activity do Tracy and Cam do on Christmas morning?

. . . .

. . . .

14. Cam gives Tracy three parcels for Christmas. Can you remember what's in all three?

. . . .

. . . .

15. What model does Tracy make for Cam's Christmas present?

. . . .

. . . .

16. What do Tracy and Cam eat for Christmas lunch?

. . . .

. . . .

THE DARE GAME

*Can you remember what happens when Tracy is
fostered by Cam but gets involved in a dangerous
game with some new friends?*

1. Tracy Beaker's teacher is called Mrs V Bagley.
What does Tracy think the V stands for?

. . . .

. . . .

2. What film does Tracy watch where the heroine says,
'There's no place like home'?

. . . .

. . . .

3. What colour paint does Tracy eventually choose for her
bedroom at Cam's house?

. . . .

. . . .

. . . .

4. And what does Cam call the room then?

....

....

5. What does Roxanne dare Tracy to tip
over her head?

....

....

6. What does Tracy see arranged in circles on a plate,
on her second visit to the empty house?

....

....

7. What job does Tracy's mum do, which
makes Tracy very proud?

....

....

8. What does Tracy find in the garden of the
empty house on her third visit, which she
takes back to its owner?

....

....

9. Which famous person is the subject of the book Alexander is reading when Tracy first meets him?

. . . .

. . . .

10. What is Alexander's first dare to Tracy?

. . . .

. . . .

11. What does Tracy take off and wave like a flag?

. . . .

. . . .

12. Where does Football dare Tracy to hang her knickers?

. . . .

. . . .

13. Where does Alexander land when he jumps out of the window?

. . . .

. . . .

14. What teasing name does Alexander get called at school?

....

....

15. What happens to Alexander when the three children are fighting?

....

....

16. Which film do Cam and Tracy watch together after Tracy's return?

....

....

☆ ☆ ☆ Quiz 4 ☆ ☆ ☆

TRACY BEAKER'S THUMPING HEART

Do you know this special extra story about Tracy and her friends at the Dumping Ground?

1. On which special day of the year does this story start?

. . . .

. . . .

2. Which little kid at the Children's Home is always making a big mess?

. . . .

. . . .

3. What is Peter always snuffling into?

. . . .

. . . .

4. Who at the Home gets the most Valentine's cards

. . . .

. . . .

5. Who is Justine's Valentine from?

....

....

6. What special present does Peter give Tracy?

....

....

7. Where does Tracy find the red velvet ribbon she uses to make a chain?

....

....

8. With which TV presenter does Tracy fall in love at first sight?

....

....

9. Which TV show is he presenting?

....

....

....

10. What do Justine and Louise decide to offer as their swap to get the karaoke machine?

. . . .

. . . .

11. What does Barney invite Tracy and the other kids to do?

. . . .

. . . .

12. Which of the kids doesn't really want to do this?

. . . .

. . . .

13. Why does Tracy decide not to go through with her swap?

. . . .

. . . .

14. How does Barney suggest the kids can win a karaoke machine?

. . . .

. . . .

15. Who does Barney make Tracy have as a partner?

. . . .

. . . .

GREEN GUNGE!

shover

rider

bed

track

tank

Scores

pointer

16. What does Tracy do to Justine at the end of the game?

. . . .

. . . .

TRACY BEAKER'S FRIENDS AND DEADLY ENEMIES

Who are Tracy's best buddies and worst foes?

1. Who was Tracy's original best friend at the Dumping Ground?

. . . .

. . . .

2. Who asks Tracy to be his friend when she helps him get dry sheets and pyjamas one night?

. . . .

. . . .

3. Who does Louise become friends with, much to Tracy's disgust?

. . . .

. . . .

. . . .

. . . .

4. What's the name of the older girl at the children's home who has a drawer full of make-up that Tracy 'borrows'?

. . . .

. . . .

5. What was the name of the little baby Tracy loved, in a Home where she used to live?

. . . .

. . . .

6. Which new friend does Tracy first meet when she comes to the home to get information for an article she's writing about children in care?

. . . .

. . . .

7. Who is the teacher who's very friendly to Tracy when she's been sent out of the classroom by Mrs V. B.?

. . . .

. . . .

. . . .

8. What's the name of the girl who gets into a fight with Tracy after teasing her because her T-shirt isn't a designer label?

. . . .

. . . .

9. What are Cam's two best friends called?

. . . .

. . . .

10. What's Tracy's name for the friend she meets when she saves his ball from whacking her in the head?

. . . .

. . . .

11. Who does Tracy discover hiding behind the curtain in the abandoned house?

. . . .

. . . .

12. Where does Tracy's mum say she's going, on the second night Tracy stays with her?

. . . .

. . . .

13. At Tracy's school, who is Trevor?

. . . .

. . . .

14. Which older boy wants Tracy to be his girlfriend?

. . . .

. . . .

15. Which three special friends does Tracy say she'd invite round to her own house when she's grown up?

. . . .

. . . .

16. What very significant thing does Cam say to Tracy, when she tells her she wants her to come back and live with her again?

. . . .

. . . .

TRACY BEAKER GETS CREATIVE!

*What do you know about Tracy's attempts
to write, draw, cook and so on?*

1. What originally gets Tracy started on writing a book?

. . . .

. . . .

2. What subject does Mrs V.B. set for story writing
that encourages Tracy to make up a long story about
a girl who escapes a crazed attacker by jumping
into a river, bumps into a corpse then sees
a strange light coming from a graveyard?

. . . .

. . . .

. . . .

3. What does Tracy create from instructions in a book by
Grizelda Moonbeam?

. . . .

. . . .

4. What drink does Tracy make for the first time, as a treat for Cam after Christmas lunch?

. . . .

. . . .

5. What does Tracy discover about making chips, at Cam's house on Christmas Day?

. . . .

. . . .

6. What does Tracy draw on the second letter she writes to Cam after meeting her?

. . . .

. . . .

. . . .

7. What does Tracy put on the breakfast table the morning after the other kids have helped her clean the Dumping Ground?

. . . .

. . . .

8. What career does Tracy think she might follow her mum into?

. . . .

. . . .

9. What part did Tracy play in the nativity play at her previous school?

. . . .

. . . .

10. When Tracy dresses up in her mum's clothes, what do she and her mum pretend to be?

. . . .

. . . .

11. What does Tracy do when she puts on the too-small designer T-shirt her mum has bought her?

. . . .

. . . .

12. What does Tracy steal from Elaine's art therapy cupboard before Christmas?

. . . .

. . . .

☆ 35 ☆

13. What's the first thing Tracy draws with the new felt-tips Cam gives her for Christmas?

. . . .

. . . .

14. What happens straightaway the first time Tracy tries ice-skating?

. . . .

. . . .

15. What sport does Tracy declare that 'Girls are great at . . .'?

. . . .

. . . .

16. What sort of thing does Tracy think Cam ought to write?

. . . .

. . . .

WHAT TRACY BEAKER WANTS . . .

*Do you know what Tracy's favourite treats
and most desperate desires are?*

1. What is Tracy Beaker's absolute favourite
thing to eat?

....

....

2. Where does Tracy want Cam to take her on their first
ever outing together?

....

....

....

3. What does E.T. in the film have that Tracy asks for too?

....

....

4. When Cam suggests a laid-back walk in the park on their first weekend together, where does Tracy persuade her to go instead?

. . . .

. . . .

5. And what cuddly toy does she get there?

. . . .

. . . .

6. What does Tracy think she needs to avoid being picked on at school by Roxanne and the other girls?

. . . .

. . . .

7. Name three things Tracy says she wants in her bedroom when Cam says she can choose how to decorate it.

. . . .

. . . .

. . . .

. . . .

8. What does Cam add when Tracy eventually chooses black paint for her bedroom?

....

....

9. What does Tracy borrow from Cam's friend Liz and then demand for herself?

....

....

10. When Elaine tells Tracy that her mum wants to see her, what does Tracy surprisingly decide at first?

....

....

11. What item of clothing does Tracy's mum buy her when she goes to live with her?

....

....

12. What does Tracy really want Football to do, the first time they meet?

....

....

13. When Tracy moves in to Cam's flat what does she want Cam to do to the bare floorboards?

. . . .

. . . .

14. What is Tracy desperate for her mum to do in *Starring Tracy Beaker*?

. . . .

. . . .

15. Which three things does Tracy tell Cam she wants for Christmas?

. . . .

. . . .

16. What do Tracy and the other kids want to bid for on *Swap Shop*, in *Tracy Beaker's Thumping Heart*?

. . . .

. . . .

'MY BOOK ABOUT ME'

*How well do you know Tracy Beaker's
life story?*

1. When is Tracy's birthday?

. . . .

. . . .

2. What does she have to share with Peter on
her birthday?

. . . .

. . . .

3. What's Tracy's school called?

. . . .

. . . .

4. What's her favourite thing to do at school?

. . . .

. . . .

5. What does Tracy *never* do?

. . . .

. . . .

6. What does Tracy say sometimes happens to make her eyes water?

. . . .

. . . .

7. What does Tracy call her social worker?

. . . .

. . . .

8. Who are the other social workers at the Dumping Ground?

. . . .

. . . .

9. Who were Tracy's first foster parents?

. . . .

. . . .

10. And which couple were her next foster parents?

. . . .

. . . .

11. Why does Tracy have to leave her second foster home?

. . . .

. . . .

12. Which special item of clothing has Tracy kept from that foster placement?

. . . .

. . . .

13. Why does Cam arrange to come to the Children's Home for a second time?

. . . .

. . . .

14. Why does Tracy usually wait by the window of the Children's Home on Saturday mornings?

....

....

15. Why is Tracy convinced she'll be such a star in the play?

....

....

16. Why does Tracy run away after she's stayed overnight with her mum?

....

....

☆ ☆ ☆ Quiz 9 ☆ ☆ ☆

TRACY BEAKER
AT SCHOOL

*Do you know what Tracy gets up to in the
classroom and the playground?*

1. What's the name of Tracy's class teacher at
Kinglea Juniors?

. . . .

. . . .

2. What colour is the school uniform?

. . . .

. . . .

3. What's the name of the art and drama
teacher who gives Tracy the main part
in the school Christmas play?

. . . .

. . . .

. . . .

4. What does Mrs Darlow, the head teacher, see when she comes through the swing doors to see the play rehearsal in the hall?

. . . .

. . . .

5. When she relents on banning Tracy from being in the school play, what other punishment does Mrs Darlow devise for her?

. . . .

. . . .

6. What does Mrs V.B. say about Tracy after she writes a very spooky story at school?

. . . .

. . . .

7. What does Tracy Beaker write about her mum when Mrs V.B. sets them an exercise in autobiography, writing about 'My Family'?

. . . .

. . . .

. . . .

. . . .

8. Where does Tracy go at playtime after Mrs V.B. has made her stand outside the classroom all morning?

. . . .

. . . .

9. Why does Tracy first end up in the back garden of the empty house?

. . . .

. . . .

10. What job does Cam's friend Liz do?

. . . .

. . . .

11. What's the name of Tracy's worst enemy at her new school, with whom she plays the Dare Game?

. . . .

. . . .

12. Why doesn't Tracy like school spaghetti bolognese?

. . . .

. . . .

13. When does Alexander bunk off school?

. . . .

. . . .

14. When Alexander is at the hospital, why does he decide he'd better stop bunking off school?

. . . .

. . . .

15. Why isn't Football at school?

. . . .

. . . .

16. What does Mr Hatherway ask Tracy to do at school?

. . . .

. . . .

☆ ☆ ☆ Quiz 10 ☆ ☆ ☆

TRACY BEAKER AND CAM

*How much do you know about Tracy's life
with her foster mum?*

1. What bad habit does Tracy notice that Cam has, the first time they meet?

. . . .

. . . .

2. What special pattern is on the socks Cam is wearing on her first visit to the Children's Home?

. . . .

. . . .

3. What's the name of the fairy Tracy draws on her second letter to Cam?

. . . .

. . . .

4. What does Tracy insist on doing after lunch on her first outing with Cam?

. . . .

. . . .

5. What does Tracy leave on Cam's desk on her first visit to her flat?

. . . .

. . . .

6. How does Cam decorate the birthday cake she buys for tea on Tracy's first visit?

. . . .

. . . .

7. What does Cam consider buying for her mum when she and Tracy go Christmas shopping?

. . . .

. . . .

8. What does Cam bring for Tracy on the night of the school play?

. . . .

. . . .

9. What does Cam do to help with the school play?

. . . .

. . . .

10. Where do Tracy and Cam have breakfast on Christmas morning?

. . . .

. . . .

11. What does Cam say is her best-ever Christmas present?

. . . .

. . . .

12. What does Cam say, much to Tracy's disappointment, when Tracy tells her she's moving out of Cam's to go and live with her mum?

. . . .

. . . .

13. What was Cam's favourite book as a child?

. . . .

. . . .

14. What's Cam's favourite film?

. . . .

. . . .

15. What do Alexander and Cam like to discuss?

. . . .

. . . .

16. Where does Alexander's dad drop Tracy off after she's had tea at his house?

. . . .

. . . .

TRACY BEAKER'S TASTY TREATS

Do you know Tracy's favourite flavours?

1. What's Tracy's very favourite thing to eat?

. . . .

. . . .

2. What's Tracy Beaker's favourite sweet?

. . . .

. . . .

3. How does Tracy disguise her midnight raid on the butter and sugar?

. . . .

. . . .

4. Where does Cam take Tracy for lunch on their first outing together?

. . . .

. . . .

5. What's Tracy's preferred flavour of milkshake?

. . . .

. . . .

6. Which milky dessert made by Aunty Peggy in her first foster placement did Tracy really hate?

. . . .

. . . .

7. What does Tracy say she put in the boots of a really tough teenager at her previous Home?

. . . .

. . . .

8. When Tracy is imagining a delicious breakfast, what does she describe as 'those puffy things with maple syrup'?

. . . .

. . . .

9. Name three of the ingredients in the recipe that Tracy finds for a 'charm to be with your loved one on a festive occasion'.

. . . .

. . . .

10. And name three items Tracy substitutes for the real ingredients.

. . . .

. . . .

11. What favourite supper does Mike bring up to Tracy's room on a tray, on the day she's had a screaming fit at school after being banned from the school play?

. . . .

. . . .

12. Where do the cast have tea on the evening of the school play?

. . . .

. . . .

. . . .

13. What do Cam and Tracy have for breakfast when they go ice-skating?

. . . .

. . . .

14. What does Cam originally suggest they have for Christmas dinner?

. . . .

. . . .

15. When Tracy buys a purple notebook what does the colour remind her of?

. . . .

. . . .

16. What is little Maxy at the Dumping Ground famous for doing with his food?

. . . .

. . . .

TRACY BEAKER'S OUTRAGEOUS DARES

How much do you know about Tracy's dangerous game?

1. When Tracy invents the Dare Game, who is the first person she dares?

. . . .

. . . .

2. And what is the first dare Tracy gives her?

. . . .

. . . .

3. What is the first dare that Justine gives Tracy?

. . . .

. . . .

4. What revolting thing do Tracy and Justine dare each other to eat?

....

....

5. What course does Tracy dare Justine to go round?

....

....

6. What does Justine dare Tracy to climb?

....

....

7. What's Tracy's first dare to Roxanne
Green at school?

....

....

8. What does Roxanne dare Tracy to do to Mrs Bagley?

. . . .

. . . .

9. What does Tracy dare Roxanne to do at break when they're in the cloakroom?

. . . .

. . . .

10. And what does Roxanne dare Tracy to do with her unwanted lunch?

. . . .

. . . .

11. What happens when Roxanne and her friends laugh at Tracy when she's done the dare?

. . . .

. . . .

12. How does Tracy persuade Alexander to answer back to the boys at school who are teasing him?

. . . .

. . . .

13. What does Alexander tell Tracy he can see after he dares her to stand on her head?

....

....

14. And what does Tracy take to be his next dare to her?

....

....

15. What is Football's first dare to Tracy?

....

....

16. What happens to Alexander when he jumps out the window after Football dares him?

....

....

☆ ☆ ☆ **Quiz 13** ☆ ☆ ☆

TRACY BEAKER'S TROUBLES

*Can you remember the worst
times for Tracy?*

1. Which allergic disease does Tracy always
blame if she has tears in her eyes?

. . . .

. . . .

2. What often happens when Tracy has a dream
about water?

. . . .

. . . .

3. Which three words does Elaine use to
describe Tracy when she puts an advert
about her in the local paper to try to find
a foster placement?

. . . .

. . . .

. . . .

4. Which words does Tracy suggest would be better?

. . . .

. . . .

5. What present did Ted and Julie give Tracy, which she destroyed when she heard she had to leave that placement?

. . . .

. . . .

6. What does Tracy do to Justine when Justine pretends to read out something from Tracy's life story book?

. . . .

. . . .

7. What does Tracy do when Cam takes her back to the Home after their first outing?

. . . .

. . . .

8. Why does Tracy's mum send her a postcard saying 'sorry'?

. . . .

. . . .

9. What did Tracy do when cast as a donkey in the school nativity play?

. . . .

. . . .

10. What miserable phrase is Scrooge in *A Christmas Carol* famous for saying?

. . . .

. . . .

11. Who comes to collect Tracy from school when she's having a screaming fit after her big fight with Justine?

. . . .

. . . .

12. What does Tracy do when Justine trips and falls flat on her face when they are performing *A Christmas Carol*?

. . . .

. . . .

13. How does the upstairs window in the abandoned house get broken when Tracy and her friends are there?

. . . .

. . . .

14. At her mum's house what does Tracy do first while her mum is asleep on the sofa?

. . . .

. . . .

15. When Tracy runs away from her mum's, where does she go?

. . . .

. . . .

16. What does Football do to Alexander's cardboard bookcase after Tracy has crumpled it all up?

. . . .

. . . .

. . . .

☆ ☆ ☆ **Quiz 14** ☆ ☆ ☆

EXTRA-TRICKY TRACY TEASERS

The toughest test for true Tracy fans

1. What is Tracy's mum's first name?

. . . .

. . . .

2. Who begs Tracy to play noughts and crosses
with him?

. . . .

. . . .

3. What sort of car does Cam have?

. . . .

. . . .

4. Which game did baby Camilla particularly like Tracy
to play with her?

. . . .

. . . .

5. What are the names of the older couple who want to foster Peter?

. . . .

. . . .

6. What's the name of the primary school to whose staff and pupils Jacqueline Wilson dedicated *Starring Tracy Beaker*?

. . . .

. . . .

7. Which part does Louise play in *A Christmas Carol*?

Louise

. . . .

. . . .

8. What does Elaine wear on her head at Christmas time?

. . . .

. . . .

9. What has one of the little kids left at the bottom of the stairs in the Children's Home, which Tracy trips over?

. . . .

. . . .

10. Why does Justine trip when she steps on stage in *A Christmas Carol*?

. . . .

. . . .

11. Why is Tracy suspicious that the bouquet of flowers she receives may not really be from her mum?

. . . .

. . . .

12. How does Elaine describe the very happy time when Tracy is first fostered by Cam?

. . . .

. . . .

13. Where is Football's dad always supposed to be taking him?

. . . .

. . . .

14. How does Tracy break Adele's black high-heeled shoes?

Oops!

. . . .

. . . .

15. Which animal co-hosts the TV programme that the kids at the Dumping Ground watch on Saturday morning?

. . . .

. . . .

16. What's the name of the game Justine and Tracy have to play to win the karaoke machine?

. . . .

. . . .

PICTURE QUIZ

*Do you recognize all these illustrations
from the books?*

1. Who is this?

. . . .

. . . .

2. Who are these people?

. . . .

. . . .

. . . .

. . . .

3. Who is this?

. . . .

. . . .

4. Who is this with Tracy?

. . . .

. . . .

5. Who is this, the owner of the make-up and shoes borrowed by Tracy?

. . . .
. . . .
. . . .
. . . .

6. Who is comforting Peter in this picture?

. . . .
. . . .
. . . .
. . . .

7. Who is this?

. . . .

. . . .

8. Who is this?

. . . .

. . . .

9. Whose bedroom is this?

. . . .

. . . .

10. Which toy is this?

. . . .

. . . .

11. Who wears these socks?

. . . .

. . . .

12. Where is this?

. . . .

. . . .

13. Where is this sofa?

. . . .

. . . .

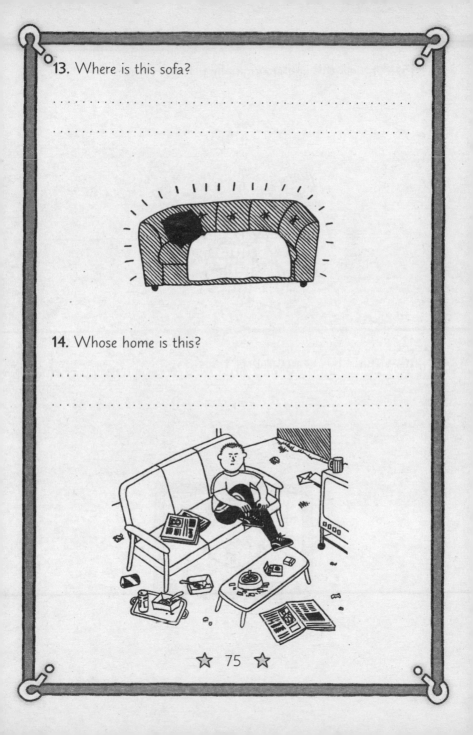

14. Whose home is this?

. . . .

. . . .

15. Who did this lighter originally belong to?

. . . .

. . . .

16. Who is this heartthrob of Tracy's?

. . . .

. . . .

TRACY BEAKER TAKES OFF . . .

*No right or wrong answers here – just a test of your
imagination. What do you think will happen to
Tracy and her friends in the future?*

1. Will Tracy pass her exams at school?

....

....

2. Will Tracy play another starring part in a school play?

....

....

3. Will Cam carry on fostering Tracy?

....

....

4. Will Tracy's mum keep in touch?

. . . .

. . . .

5. Will Tracy ever visit her mum's
house again?

. . . .

. . . .

6. Will Tracy stay in touch with Alexander?

. . . .

. . . .

. . . .

7. Will Football stay in touch with Tracy?

. . . .

. . . .

8. Will Peter get adopted?

. . . .

. . . .

. . . .

9. Will Justine and Louise continue to be best friends?

....

....

10. What will Tracy do when she leaves school?

....

....

11. What will Tracy's first job be?

....

....

12. Will Tracy ever get married?

....

....

THUMP
Tracy's heart
THUMP THUMP

13. Will Tracy ever have a baby?

. . . .

. . . .

14. Will Tracy realize her ambition to
become a famous writer?

. . . .

. . . .

. . . .

15. What amazing secret might Tracy discover one day?

. . . .

. . . .

16. Which fabulous place might Tracy visit in the future?

. . . .

. . . .

☆ ☆ ☆ TRACY'S TOP TIPS! ☆ ☆ ☆

Forced to clean and tidy up around your home?
Blast out your favourite music while you're doing it —
and best of all, get your mates to help!

Had a terrible row with a good friend?
Clear the air by being there when
they need you!

☆ ☆ ☆

Teacher thinks you're bottom of the class?
Knock her socks off with your best-ever
piece of no-holds-barred imaginative
creative writing.

Someone making you feel small?
Go and see someone different,
who knows you're great!

**Regretting something silly
you've done?**
Make a peace offering.

☆ ☆ ☆ MAKE A TRACY ☆ ☆ ☆ TOKEN

When Cam receives a book token for Christmas in
Starring Tracy Beaker, it gives Tracy the idea of making
her a Tracy token. With a book token you can go
to any bookshop and choose whichever book you like,
up to the value of the token. With a Tracy token,
Tracy promises all sorts of treats for Cam.

*'I, Tracy Beaker promise to make you a plate of my
famous egg and chips whenever I'm round at your
place . . . If I get to be a famous writer I'll dedicate
my first book to you . . . and if you finish your
classes and go through with fostering me I will
be the best foster daughter ever.'*

Brighten up the birthday or Christmas of your best friend, dad, mum, granny, sister or other special person with their own unique gift token.

☆ HERE'S HOW: ☆

1. Take a piece of card at least 24cm x 17cm. Fold it in half.

2. On the front, give your token a special name. Try to use the name to show who it is from or who it's for. Is it a ' Tess Token', a 'Grace Gift', a 'Polly Promise' or a 'Vicky Voucher'? Or is it a 'Mum's Day Off Token', a 'Little Sister's Homework Helper Token' or a 'Grandad's Garden Assistant Voucher'?

3. Decorate the front with a picture showing how the token can be used. Brighten it up with vibrant colours, stuck-on jewels, feathers, foam shapes etc.

4. Write out the message inside in your best handwriting, to explain what the token is for and what you're offering to do for the lucky recipient.

☆ ☆ ☆ THE DARE GAME ☆ ☆ ☆ PLAY!

If you and your friends are budding actresses, just like Tracy, why not have a bit of fun acting out some scenes from the books? Did you know that Jacqueline Wilson originally wrote *The Dare Game* as a play before turning it into a novel? To get you started, here's a scene from *The Dare Game* when Tracy, Alexander and Football are all hanging out at the abandoned house. No need for fancy costumes, props or scenery; learn from Tracy and use the power of your imagination!

TRACY: I *have* to bunk off school one more time. To see how little old Alexander is doing. Maybe he's learnt to stand up for himself. *Maybe.* [*Tracy goes to the derelict house, climbs in the kitchen window and starts shouting.*] Alexander! Alexander! [*Disappointed*] Alexander's not here.

ALEXANDER [*coming on stage, in very small voice*]: Yes I am.

TRACY: There you are! Were you hiding from me again?

ALEXANDER: No. I was just upstairs.

TRACY: So? How did you get on at school? You know, with the big bully boys in the showers?

ALEXANDER [*despairing*]: The entire school calls me Gherkin now.

TRACY [*trying not to giggle*]: Oh dear.

ALEXANDER: It didn't work. It's made things much worse.

TRACY: Never mind.

ALEXANDER: But I do mind. Dreadfully.

TRACY: Still. At least you won the dare. I mean I dared you to do it. And you did. So you get to win that dare.

ALEXANDER [*sadly*]: Big deal.

TRACY: OK. You get to dare me now.

ALEXANDER: I don't really want to, thank you.

TRACY: Yes you do!

ALEXANDER: I can't make up any dares. *You* make one up, Tracy.

TRACY: Oh, don't be so wet. Come on. Dare me to do something really really wicked.

ALEXANDER: All right. I dare you to . . . I dare you to . . . stand on your head.

TRACY [*exasperated*]: Easy peasy! [*She does*]

ALEXANDER: Gosh. You're good at it.

TRACY: *Anyone* can stand on their head.

ALEXANDER: I can't.

TRACY: I might have known. Look. It's simple. [*She demonstrates*]

ALEXANDER [*giggling*]: I can see your knickers.

TRACY: Well, don't look.

ALEXANDER: I can't help it. [*Singing*] 'Leap up and down and wave your knickers in the air!'

TRACY (*Right way up again*): You what?

ALEXANDER: It's a song. My dad sings in when he's in a good mood. Which isn't often when I'm around.

TRACY: Is that another dare? OK. [*Tracy takes off her knickers and leaps*

☆ 85 ☆

up and down, waving them in the air]
ALEXANDER [Giggling, shocked, delighted and embarrassed]: Tracy! *Um!*
[*Tracy hams it up even more, leaping around and waving her knickers wildly in front of the window.*]
Tracy! Get away from the window.
[*Tracy leaps and waves*]
TRACY: I don't care. Look at me, everyone! Look at me-e-e-e-e!
[*A football comes flying through the window and bounces across the floor.*] Whoops!
ALEXANDER: A football! I wonder who on Earth threw it in here?
TRACY: Three guesses!
[*Football himself climbs through the window*]
TRACY [*bouncing the ball with one hand*]: Right, right, right!
FOOTBALL: Give me that ball back, Curly Bonce!
TRACY: Finders keepers.
FOOTBALL: Give it here!
TRACY: It's my house. So it's my football now.
FOOTBALL: It's not your house.
TRACY [*bouncing ball*]: It *is.*
ALEXANDER [*trying to be assertive*]: It's my house too!
[*Football flattens him with one hand, barely trying*]
TRACY: Hey, leave the little guy alone.
FOOTBALL: Or else?
TRACY [*waving wildly*]: Else I'll flatten you!
FOOTBALL: You're a right little joker, aren't you? What's that you're waving? A hankie?

TRACY [*embarrassed*]: Mmm — yes.

FOOTBALL: It's your *knickers*! What're you doing with your knickers off, you naughty little girl?

ALEXANDER: She's leaping up and down and waving her knickers in the air.

TRACY: Shut *up*, Alexander.

FOOTBALL: Well, feel free, Curly Bonce.

[*Football starts kicking his football round, aiming it at Tracy and Alexander. Tracy kicks it straight back, harder. Alexander messes things up. Football groans.*]

TRACY: Look, do you mind? You're kicking that ball round my living room.

ALEXANDER [*quietly*]: And *my* living room.

FOOTBALL: Well, it's *my* living room too, and if I want to turn it into and indoor football pitch I shall. [*He starts dribbling it around.*] Here's Football, ready to save the day, yes, he intercepts the ball brilliantly, heading it straight into the net! I've never seen such a brilliant goal!

TRACY: How old are you — six? Sad little kid.

FOOTBALL [*kicking the ball at her harder than usual*]: You wait till I'm famous!

TRACY: I bet I'll be heaps more famous than you.

FOOTBALL: Women footballers are rubbish.

TRACY: Not football, you nutcase. I'm going to be a famous actress, like my mum.

FOOTBALL: Now who's the sad little kid? Famous actress! [*Football bounces the ball too near Alexander, making him duck.*] You going to be a famous actress too?

TRACY: He's going to be famous, he's dead brainy, top of everything at school. He could go on all the quiz shows on the telly and know every single answer. You could have a special telly name. Alexander isn't exactly catchy. How about Brainbox?

ALEXANDER: They call me that at school. And other stuff. [*He droops.*] And my dad calls me Mr Clever Dick.

TRACY: I don't think I like the sound of your dad, Alexander.

FOOTBALL: *My* dad's the best ever.

TRACY: I haven't got a dad so I don't know whether he's the best or the worst. I've got a mum though. You'll never guess what! She's going to take me to live at her place — it's dead luxurious, all gilt and mirrors and chandeliers and rich ruby red — and she's going to buy me new clothes, designer stuff, and new trainers, and a brand-new computer and my own telly and video and a bike and pets and we're going on heaps of trips to Disneyland and I bet we won't even have to queue because my mum's such a famous actress—

FOOTBALL: What's her name then?

TRACY: Carly. Carly Beaker.

FOOTBALL: Never heard of her.

TRACY: Oh well. That's not her acting name.

FOOTBALL: Which is . . . ?

TRACY: Sharon Stone.

FOOTBALL: If your mum's Sharon Stone my dad's Alan Shearer.

ALEXANDER: What, Alan Shearer's your dad? No wonder you're good at football.

FOOTBALL [*to Tracy*]: I thought he was supposed to be bright? Anyway, my dad's better than Alan Shearer. We're like that, my dad and me. [*Gesturing with linked fingers*] We do all sorts together. Well. We did.

TRACY: Past tense?

FOOTBALL: Well. He's got his girlfriend. And my mum found out and now my dad's gone off with this girlfriend. And I don't blame him. I mean, Mum just nags and moans and gives him a hard time — but Dad says it doesn't mean we're not still mates.

ALEXANDER [*enviously*]: So your dad doesn't live with you any more?

FOOTBALL: But we still do all sorts of stuff together. And we always go to the match together. Well, Dad couldn't make it this time — and last time — because he's still, like, sorting out his new life — but he's taking me *next* time, he's promised. [*Football feels in his pocket and proudly brings out a lighter.*] Look!

TRACY: Ooh, good, have you got a fag?

FOOTBALL: I don't smoke. It's bad for my football, right? No, this is my *dad's* lighter. See the make? It's not one of your tacky throw-away sort. It's *gold*.

ALEXANDER: Solid gold!

FOOTBALL: Well. Plated. Still cost a fortune. It's my dad's most precious possession. His mates gave it to him for his twenty-first birthday. He's never without it, my dad.

TRACY: He seems to be without it now.

FOOTBALL: That's the point. He's given it to me.

[*Football flicks it on and off.*]

TRACY: You'll be waving it around at a rock concert next.

FOOTBALL: You shut your face, Curly Bonce. You haven't even *got* a dad.

ALEXANDER: I wish I didn't. Or I wish my dad would go off with a girlfriend. I wish wishes could come true. What would you wish for, Football? That you and your dad could be together?

FOOTBALL: Mmm. And to play for United.

ALEXANDER: What about you, Tracy?

TRACY: I don't want a dad.

ALEXANDER: What about your mum?

TRACY: My mum . . .

ALEXANDER: Would you wish you and your mum could be together?

TRACY: Well, that would be wasted, wouldn't it, because I'm going to be with her *anyway*, aren't I?

☆ ☆ ☆ TRACY'S WICKED WORD SEARCH

Can you find Tracy and nine of her friends?

K	L	U	Q	R	J	H	H	I	I	U
Q	O	E	P	E	T	E	R	K	R	N	U
V	U	J	Q	I	O	V	A	B	J	E	D
F	I	U	C	E	O	F	P	D	B	K	I
V	S	S	X	A	V	B	F	L	E	C	A
D	E	T	B	W	M	M	Z	G	E	L	J
K	Q	I	G	A	A	S	P	P	S	H	E
M	F	N	C	Y	C	T	T	R	A	C	Y
C	T	E	A	N	F	V	O	M	I	K	E
T	S	S	P	E	E	G	O	R	A	W	E
X	B	J	E	N	N	Y	M	A	X	Y	V
D	P	J	B	S	T	F	E	N	P	A	J

TRACY   CAM   JUSTINE   LOUISE
ADELE   JENNY   MIKE   MAXY
PETER   WAYNE

☆ ☆ ☆ CAM LAWSON'S ☆ ☆ ☆ TOP TEN SUPER READS!

**These are the books Cam gives Tracy for Christmas
and this is what she tells Tracy about them:**

☆ *Little Women* ☆

It's about this family of sisters and they like acting too,
and reading Charles Dickens. You'll especially like Jo,
who's a tomboy and wants to be a writer.

☆ *Black Beauty* ☆

It's a wonderful story, and there's a very sad
bit about a horse called Ginger which always
makes me cry, but it's lovely all the same.

☆ *What Katy Did* ☆

This is about a big family — Katy's the eldest and she's
always in heaps of trouble but then she falls off a swing
and she can't walk for ages. She's got a very saintly
cousin who irritates a bit, but it's a great story, truly.

☆ *The Wind in the Willows* ☆

This is about a mole and a rat who are great chums
and they have this pal Toad who's a terrible
show-off, and there are some very
funny bits.

☆ *Five Children and It* ☆

It's about these kids who meet a sand fairy and all their wishes come true, but they always go wrong.

☆ *Mary Poppins* ☆

The book's much better than the film.

☆ *Tom Sawyer* ☆

I love this because Tom's very badly behaved and always in trouble.

☆ *Anne of Green Gables* ☆

It's all about this little orphan girl who won't ever stop talking. You'll identify big time with these last two!

☆ *The Secret Garden* ☆

I'm sure you'll like this because Mary is wondrously grouchy and rude to everyone and has to live in a house with a hundred rooms on the Yorkshire Moors.

☆ *Ballet Shoes* ☆

This is a perfect book for you, because these three sisters want to go to a stage school and perform in lots of plays.

☆ ☆ ☆ TRACY'S TERRIFIC ☆ ☆ ☆ HOME-MADE BURGERS

Tracy may not be famous for her skills in the kitchen but she does love to tuck away a good burger and what could be tastier than a home-made one! It's as easy as pie — in fact, a pie would be a lot harder! Just follow these simple instructions to make enough for four or five people.

☆ INGREDIENTS ☆

500g minced beef
small onion, finely chopped (optional)
salt and pepper
1 egg, beaten
1 slice bread, crusts cut off, soaked in water
or large handful breadcrumbs

1. Put the mince in a mixing bowl and add the onion if using. Add the beaten egg and the bread or breadcrumbs. Season with salt and pepper.

2. Stir vigorously with a wooden spoon to soften the meat and mix everything together.

3. Use your hands to shape into 4 large burgers or 6 smaller ones.

4. Brush the surface of the burgers with a tiny bit of sunflower or olive oil.

5. With adult help, heat the grill or a cast-iron ridged grill pan till very hot. Put the burgers under the grill or on the grill pan. Turn over after about 5 minutes, and cook about another 5 minutes. The outside should have dark stripes while the inside is pinker and more juicy.

6. Serve on split burger buns with lashings of ketchup and salad on the side, or however you like.

Enjoy!

burger →

yum!

☆ ☆ ☆ TRACY AND ☆ ☆ ☆ FOOTBALL'S SOCCER SKILLS

I'm Tracy-Superstar, the girl-goalie with nanosecond-quick reactions. I leapt, I clutched, I tucked the ball close to my chest — saved!

Warm up, get into practice and play like a pro — just like Tracy and Football reckon they can. Here are some exercises to hone your skills.

☆ KEEPY-UPPY ☆

Everybody's favourite football challenge! How long can you keep the ball in the air using only your feet, legs and head? Did you know the world record is over 19 hours?

☆ ALTERNATE FEET ☆

Dribble your football forward using alternate feet, one touch at a time. First your left foot is on the ball, next your right and so on. Time yourself over a fixed distance; try to improve your times or compete against a buddy. Then double the difficulty and do it going backwards!

'Superb tackle! The great Tracy Beaker and her brilliant footwork yet again. She's really come good, this girl . . .'

☆ PIGGY IN THE MIDDLE ☆

A footie version of the classic catching game. Play with two friends. One person must stand in the middle. The other two must try to pass the ball to each other without letting the middle player trap it. If she does, then the player who lost the ball must change places and go in the middle. Practice different passes using the 'laces' part of your foot and the inside of your foot.

☆ HEADING THE BALL ☆

One of the trickiest skills to master — but brilliantly useful in a match. Easier for those with height and tougher nuts, like Football himself, but everyone can have a go if they remember these tips:

Always use the middle of your forehead to head the ball, never the top or sides of your head. When preparing for a header, have your feet firmly and steadily on the ground, relax your body and keep your eyes on the ball. Lean back slightly as the ball drops towards you, then use your feet to push your head up towards the ball.

☆ ☆ ☆ PETER'S PEN AND ☆ ☆ ☆ PAPER GAMES

Peter always used to play pen and paper games with his nan and he persuades Tracy Beaker to play with him too. Simple, fun and quick, even Tracy admits paper games are a good way to pass the time. All you need is a piece of paper, a pencil or pen and one friend to play with you. Just in case you've never played before, like Tracy until she met Peter, here are some easy instructions.

☆ NOUGHTS AND CROSSES ☆

Use a grid with 9 spaces, like the ones below. One player uses noughts and one player uses crosses. Take it in turns to draw your symbol in one of the boxes. The first player to create a row of three — horizontally, vertically or diagonally — is the winner.

☆ CONSEQUENCES ☆

This can be played with more than two people. Each player needs a piece of paper, preferably quite long and not too wide, like a shopping list. Each player writes a male name at top of their paper. It can be anyone — a friend, classmate, relative, famous footballer, popstar, politician etc. Everyone must fold the paper over so the name is hidden, then write the word 'met' beneath the fold. Pass your paper to the player on your left, so everyone ends up with a new piece of paper. Now, without looking at the name already on the paper, write a female name, followed by 'at'. Fold the paper over again to hide the second name and pass to your left. Write a location on the new piece of paper received — think of somewhere interesting, exotic, surprising or just everyday. Fold the paper over then write the words 'He said'. Pass it on again. Think up a sentence someone might have said and write it down. Fold the paper over, write 'She said' and pass the paper to your left. Write down another sentence, fold the paper, write 'Then they' and pass it on again. Write a descriptive sentence about what might have happened — let your imagination run wild. Has your 'couple' argued, fallen in love, invented something, run away somewhere, been kidnapped by aliens, been chosen to star in a new reality TV show etc etc? Finally, pass the paper on once more, unfold the one you receive and take turns in reading them out.

Prepare for a serious attack of the giggles!

☆ HANGMAN ☆

One player thinks of a word and draws dashes on the paper to show how many letters are in it. The other player must try to guess the word, one letter at a time. Correct guesses are filled in on the dashes; incorrect letters are written down below. For each incorrect letter one line of a picture of a gallows and a hanging body is drawn. The guesser must try to decipher the word before the complete picture is drawn and she is hanged!

_ A _ _ I L L A   L A _ _ _ O N

B K U D E Y J P
T R Y

☆ BOXES ☆

Draw a grid of dots, six by six, as shown on the next page. Take it in turns to draw a line linking two consecutive dots, horizontally or vertically. The aim is to form a box with four sides drawn in. The person who draws the fourth line which completes a box claims it as hers by writing her initial inside it. When the grid is as full of boxes as possible, count how many belong to each player. The player with the most boxes is the winner. You can start with a larger grid (e.g. 10 dots by 10) if you want the game to last longer.

☆ ☆ ☆ SMARTIE FAIRY CAKES

Tracy Beaker's two favourite treats are cake and Smarties – combine the two with this easy recipe to make a very sweet treat! *(Makes 12)*

☆ INGREDIENTS FOR THE CAKES ☆
100g soft margarine or butter
100g caster sugar
2 eggs
100g self-raising flour
1 teaspoon vanilla essence
12 fairy cake cases

☆ INGREDIENTS FOR THE ICING: ☆
225g icing sugar
about 2 tablespoons water
1 tube Smarties

yum!

☆ METHOD ☆

1. Preheat the oven to 180°C/ Gas Mark 4.
Cream the margarine (or butter) and sugar together
in a large mixing bowl, till light and fluffy.

2. Beat in the eggs one at a time.

3. Beat in 1 tablespoon of flour.

4. Add the vanilla essence and fold in the rest
of the flour.

5. Line a fairy cake tin with paper cases and half-fill
each case with the mixture.

6. Get an adult to help put the tin in the oven and
bake for 20 minutes till risen and slightly golden.

7. Remove and cool on a wire rack.

8. When cakes are cool, mix the icing sugar with
enough water (about 2 tablespoons) to allow it
to spread easily without being too runny. Spread
on each fairy cake and immediately decorate with
Smarties. You can make a face or spell out your
friends' initials, as Cam did on the birthday cake
she bought for Tracy on their first outing.

☆ ☆ ☆ TRACY'S TRICKSTER ☆ ☆ ☆ CROSSWORD

Tracy Beaker is more famous for cross words than crosswords, but see if you can solve this one!

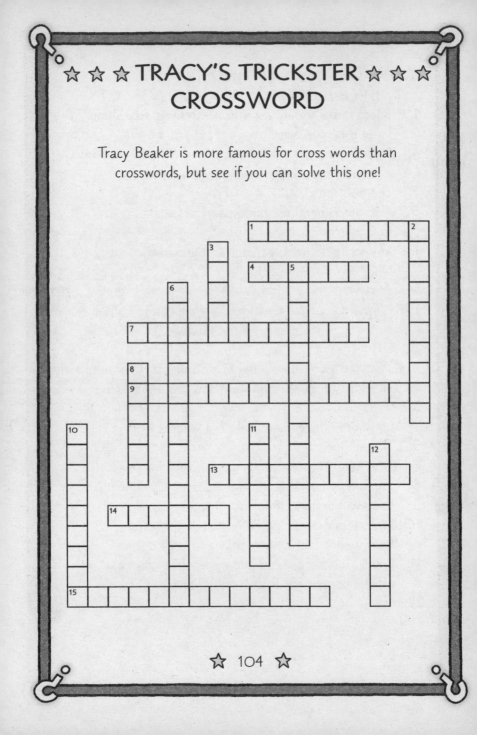

☆ ACROSS ☆

1. Meat Patty, usually served on a sesame seed bun, loved by Tracy Beaker
4. Necklace charm that can open to hold a small photo, as given to Tracy by Peter
7. The illustrator of the Tracy Beaker Books
9. The full name of the character Tracy play in *A Christmas Carol*
13. Winter sport tried by Cam and Tracy on Christmas Morning
14. Tracy's original best friend at the Children's Home
15. Nickname for the Children's Home

☆ DOWN ☆

2. The sort of fierce dog Tracy thinks she'd like
3. What Tracy does by the window when she thinks her mum is coming
5. The author of *A Christmas Carol*
6. The author of the Tracy Beaker books
8. The creepy-crawly nickname that Tracy gives to Peter in the first book
10. Film capital of the USA, where Tracy thinks her mum might be working
11. Small pickled cucumber, and Tracy's unfortunate nickname for Alexander
12. Tracy hangs these on a fir tree in *The Dare Game*

THE STORY
OF TRACY BEAKER

1. Her life story book, MY BOOK ABOUT ME

2. Bluebell

3. Mickey Mouse

4. He's trying to sort out wet sheets from his bed.

5. She puts on make-up and plaits her hair.

6. The Quiet Room

7. Worms

8. They share the same birthday – 8 May.

9. Pen and paper games, e.g. noughts and crosses.

10. Justine and Louise

11. Her dad

12. Yes, a rabbit named Lettuce

13. A white minivan

14. A Cadillac

15. ET

16. The Mickey Mouse pen that Cam has given her.

STARRING
TRACY BEAKER

1. A Christmas Carol

2. Scrooge

3. It's a magic spell to try to ensure she spends Christmas with her mum.

4. A pink lipstick, handcream, a heart necklace and a paperback copy of *A Christmas Carol*

5. Tracy punches Justine in the nose.

6. Appearing in the school play

7. The cleaning

8. Peter

9. He organises a petition.

10. School shirt, grey trousers and a raincoat cut to look like a tailcoat; a white nightshirt, nightcap and slippers

11. Tiny Tim

12. A bouquet of flowers

13. Ice-skating

14. Books; art supplies; a silver star pin

15. A model of Tracy Beaker

16. Egg and chips

THE DARE GAME

1. Vomit

2. *The Wizard of Oz*

3. Black

4. The bat cave

5. Spaghetti bolognese

6. Smarties

7. Actress

8. A football

9. Alexander the Great

10. He dares Tracy to stand on her head.

11. Her knickers!

12. On the fir tree

13. On an old mattress in the garden

14. Gherkin

15. He breaks his leg

16. The Piano

TRACY BEAKER'S THUMPING HEART

1. Valentine's Day

2. Maxy

3. His special hankie that belonged to his nan

4. Adele

5. Her dad

6. His nan's gold heart locket

7. Threaded through a blouse belonging to Adele

8. Barney (Harwood)

9. Swap Shop

10. A hair-straightening kit

11. To come into the studio and be on TV

12. Peter

13. Because she knows Peter will be really upset if she gives away his nan's heart locket

14. By taking part in the Gungulator game

15. Justine

16. She pushes her into the green slimy gunge!

TRACY BEAKER'S FRIENDS AND DEADLY ENEMIES

1. Louise
2. Peter
3. Justine Littlewood
4. Adele
5. Camilla
6. Cam Lawson
7. Mr Hatherway
8. Roxanne Green
9. Jane and Liz
10. Football
11. Alexander
12. To the karaoke evening at the pub with some friends
13. He's the smallest boy in Year Three and Mr Hatherway asks Tracy to keep an eye on him at playtime to stop him being picked on.
14. Football
15. Football, Alexander and Cam
16. 'I love you.'

TRACY BEAKER GETS CREATIVE!

1. Elaine gives her a life story book to fill in, called MY BOOK ABOUT ME.

2. 'Night-time'

3. A charm to be with a loved one on a festive occasion.

4. A cup of tea

5. She finds out that you have to peel and cut up potatoes to make chips – not just get them out the freezer as they do at the Children's Home!

6. Goblinda the goblin, spitting on some fairies

7. A thank-you card she has drawn

8. Acting

9. A donkey

10. Rock stars

11. She shows off her belly button and dances.

12. Pink tissue, white card and felt-tip pens, to wrap presents and write cards for her mum.

13. A Tracy token

14. She slips over onto her bottom!

15. Football

16. Bestselling novels

WHAT TRACY BEAKER WANTS . . .

1. Birthday cake

2. McDonald's

3. Smarties

4. To Chessington World of Adventures (a theme park)

5. A snake

6. Designer clothes

7. Any three from: king-size bed with white satin duvet; dressing table with lights around the mirror; sound system; computer; white carpet; white television and video; circus trapeze; ensuite bathroom.

8. Luminous silver stars

9. Rollerblades

10. She decides that she doesn't want to see her mum.

11. Combat trousers

12. Play football with her

13. Cover the floor with carpet

14. To come and see her in the school play.

15. Designer jeans, a furry jacket with a hood and a motorized go-cart

16. A karaoke machine

☆ ☆ ☆ Answers to Quiz 8 ☆ ☆ ☆

'MY BOOK ABOUT ME'

1. 8 May

2. The birthday cake

3. Kinglea Junior School

4. Story writing

5. Cry

6. She has an attack of hayfever.

7. Elaine the Pain

8. Mike and Jenny

9. Aunty Peggy and Uncle Sid

10. Julie and Ted

11. Julie and Ted are expecting their own baby and they're worried that Tracy wouldn't deal very well with it!

12. A hand-knitted mohair sweater with 'Tracy' in bright blue letters on it

13. To interview Tracy

14. To see if her mum is coming to visit

15. Because she says her mum is a Hollywood actress

16. Because she overhears her mum making arrangements to get rid of Tracy the following weekend so she can go to the races with her boyfriend

TRACY AT SCHOOL

1. Miss Brown

2. Grey

3. Miss Simpkins

4. She sees Tracy punch Justine in the nose.

5. She has to clean and polish the hall floor.

6. She says she has a very warped imagination.

7. She writes that her mum is an actress starring in a Hollywood movie with George Clooney etc.

8. She bunks off school and wanders the streets.

9. Because she's dying for a wee and she hops over the wall to relieve herself in the garden!

10. She's a teacher.

11. Roxanne Green

12. Because the cook makes it bright red like blood and the spaghetti seems extra-wiggly like worms

13. On the days he has games or PE

14. Because he decides he might become a doctor so he needs to go to school and pass his exams.

15. Because he's been excluded

16. To look after Trevor, a boy in Year Three who is being bullied

☆ ☆ ☆ **Answers to Quiz 10** ☆ ☆ ☆

TRACY BEAKER
AND CAM

1. She bites her fingernails.

2. A pattern of books

3. Goblinda

4. She phones the Children's Home, to make sure her mum hasn't turned up.

5. A typed note

6. She spells out 'TB' in Smarties.

7. A fake pearl necklace

8. A big box of chocolates

9. She does all the stage make-up.

10. In the park, by the skating rink

11. Her 'Tracy token'

12. She says nothing!

13. *Little Women*

14. *The Piano*

15. Books

16. Cam's home

TRACY BEAKER'S TASTY TREATS

1. Birthday cake

2. Smarties

3. She makes weeny lines like teeth marks and little paw prints all over the butter so Jenny will think a mouse has eaten it.

4. McDonald's

5. Strawberry

6. Tapioca pudding

7. Custard

8. Waffles

9. Three from: mead, dandelion wine, cinnamon, ginger, sugar.

10. Three from: honey, wine, dandelion, ginger biscuits.

11. Spaghetti bolognese

12. They have a picnic sitting on the hall floor.

13. Croissants and hot chocolate

14. Tofu and vegetable casserole

15. A bar of Cadbury's milk chocolate

16. Making a terrible mess!

TRACY BEAKER'S OUTRAGEOUS DARES

1. Justine

2. She dares her to say the rudest word she can think of when the vicar comes to visit.

3. She dares her to go out in the garden stark naked.

4. Worms

5. A skateboard assault course she's made in the garden

6. The tree at the end of the garden

7. To say a rude word to Mrs Bagley, their teacher

8. To stick her tongue out at her

9. To run into the boys' toilets

10. To tip it over her head

11. Tracy tips Roxanne's lunch over her head!

12. She dares him to do it, and says he's got to do it if he wants to be her friend.

13. Her knickers

14. To wave her knickers in the air

15. To jump into the fir tree and hang her knickers over one of the branches

16. He falls into the garden and lands on a mattress.

☆ ☆ ☆ Answers to Quiz 13 ☆ ☆ ☆

TRACY BEAKER'S TROUBLES

1. Hay fever

2. She wets the bed

3. Lively, healthy, chatty

4. Brilliant and beautiful

5. A bike

6. She punches her in the nose and makes it bleed.

7. She has a tantrum because she doesn't want to go back and she ends up in the Quiet Room.

8. Because she didn't turn up when she was supposed to take Tracy out for the day

9. She 'eeyored' constantly throughout the whole performance.

10. 'Bah, humbug!'

11. Jenny

12. She saves the day by improvising a couple of lines of script and hauling Justine to her feet.

13. Football kicks his ball and it bounces off the opposite wall and breaks the window.

14. She empties the ashtrays and clears up the glasses and empty bottles.

15. To the abandoned house.

16. He sets fire to it.

EXTRA TRICKY
TRACY TEASERS

1. Carly

2. Peter

3. A grass-green Citroen

4. The finger family

5. Auntie Vi and Uncle Stanley

6. Charles Dickens Primary School

7. The Ghost of Christmas Past

8. Rainbow reindeer antlers on a hairband

9. Some plastic dinosaurs

10. Because she looks out at her dad in the audience

11. Because the writing on the card is not her mum's handwriting

12. A honeymoon period

13. To a football match on Saturday

14. By stamping in them while pretending to be a Spanish dancer

15. Basil Brush

16. The Gungulator

PICTURE QUIZ

1. Tracy's mum, Carly Beaker, holding baby Tracy

2. Julie and Ted, who fostered Tracy

3. Elaine, Tracy's social worker

4. Miss Simpkins, the drama teacher

5. Adele

6. Mike, the care worker at the Home

7. Football's mum

8. Mrs Darlow, the head teacher

9. Cam's

10. Bluebell

11. Cam

12. The Dumping Ground, or Children's Home

13. In the living room of the abandoned house

14. Football's

15. Football's dad

16. Barney Harwood

☆ ☆ ☆ TRACY'S WICKED ☆ ☆ ☆
WORD SEARCH SOLUTION

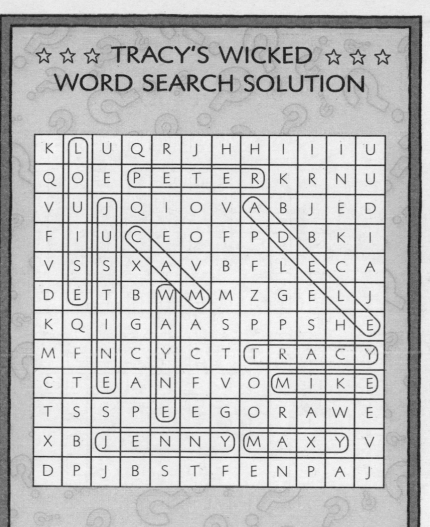

K	L	U	Q	R	J	H	H	I	I	I	U
Q	O	E	P	E	T	E	R	K	R	N	U
V	U	J	Q	I	O	V	A	B	J	E	D
F	I	U	C	E	O	F	P	D	B	K	I
V	S	S	X	A	V	B	F	L	E	C	A
D	E	T	B	W	M	M	Z	G	E	L	J
K	Q	I	G	A	A	S	P	P	S	H	E
M	F	N	C	Y	C	T	T	R	A	C	Y
C	T	E	A	N	F	V	O	M	I	K	E
T	S	S	P	E	E	G	O	R	A	W	E
X	B	J	E	N	N	Y	M	A	X	Y	V
D	P	J	B	S	T	F	E	N	P	A	J

☆ ☆ ☆ TRACY'S TRICKSTER ☆ ☆ ☆ CROSSWORD SOLUTION

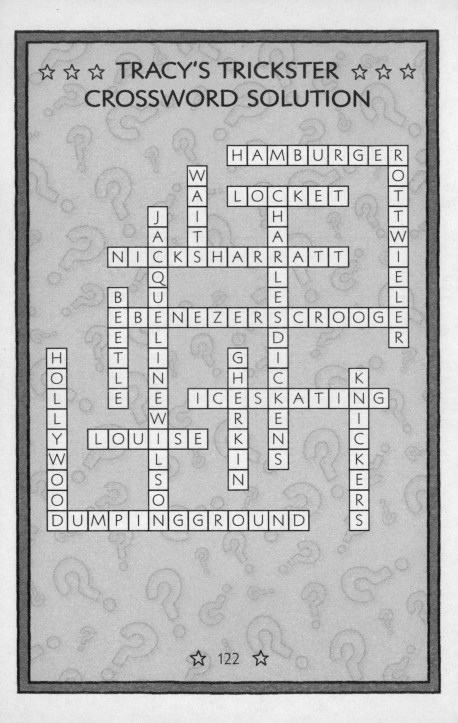

☆ ☆ ☆ SCORE SHEETS ☆ ☆ ☆

Record your scores here; one point for each correct answer, and maybe half a point for very nearly right, at the discretion of your quiz master! Remember, there are no right or wrong answers for quiz 16 but why not vote on who has the best answer and award points accordingly? More score sheets on the following pages so you can play more than once and try to improve your score, or do the quizzes again with different friends.

☆ ☆ ☆ SCORE SHEET ☆ ☆ ☆

	Name	Name	Name	Name	Name
Quiz Number					
1					
2					
3					
4					
5					
6					
7					
8					
9					
10					
11					
12					
13					
14					
15					
16					
Total					

☆ ☆ ☆ SCORE SHEET ☆ ☆ ☆

	Name	Name	Name	Name	Name
Quiz Number					
1					
2					
3					
4					
5					
6					
7					
8					
9					
10					
11					
12					
13					
14					
15					
16					
Total					

☆ ☆ ☆ SCORE SHEET ☆ ☆ ☆

	Name	Name	Name	Name	Name
Quiz Number					
1					
2					
3					
4					
5					
6					
7					
8					
9					
10					
11					
12					
13					
14					
15					
16					
Total					

☆ ☆ ☆ SCORE SHEET ☆ ☆ ☆

	Name	Name	Name	Name	Name
Quiz Number					
1					
2					
3					
4					
5					
6					
7					
8					
9					
10					
11					
12					
13					
14					
15					
16					
Total					

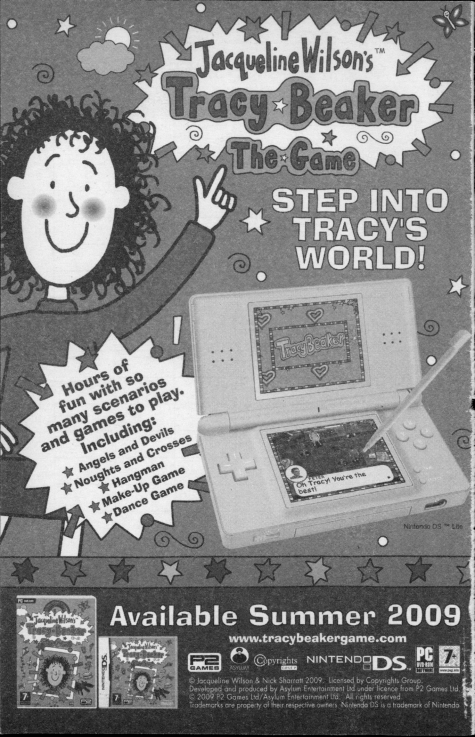